CONTENTS

The FTM Handbook
B. Hayes

TABLE OF CONTENTS

CHAPTER ONE: INTRODUCTION

Part One: Understanding Transgender Identity

What does transgender *really* mean? In our increasingly politicized environment, the connotation regarding the word 'transgender' has become muddled. Transgender people are individuals whose gender identity differs from the sex they were assigned at birth. In simple terms, they may be born with physical characteristics typically associated with either male or female, but their internal sense of self and gender identity does not align with that assigned sex. A transgender person is anyone who does not identify with their birth sex. I, for example, am transgender. I was born female and transitioned to male. The term transgender also accounts for non-binary folks, as they don't identify with their birth sex.

When humans are born, the first thing doctors do is determine the sex. This is what we call one's assigned gender at birth, or AGAB. The thing is, your AGAB may not always align with your gender identity. When someone is uncomfortable with their AGAB, that's called gender dysphoria. The majority of transgender people experience this in one way or another. Conversely, many transgender people feel gender euphoria when able to present

A transgender person may choose to socially and medically transition, or they may forego the medical aspect. Social transition refers to changing names, pronouns, and being regarded as your desired gender. Medical transition refers to things such as HRT, also known as hormone replacement therapy, and surgical intervention. Not every trans person chooses to pursue medical transition.

It is crucial to recognize and respect a person's gender identity and use the correct name and pronouns they prefer.

Misgendering (using the wrong pronouns or referring to someone by their assigned sex rather than their true gender) can be hurtful and invalidating to transgender individuals.

It is also essential to distinguish between gender identity and sexual orientation. Gender identity is about who a person knows themselves to be (e.g., man, woman, non-binary, genderqueer), while sexual orientation is about who a person is attracted to romantically or sexually (e.g., heterosexual, homosexual, bisexual).

As with any diverse group of people, transgender individuals have a wide range of experiences, perspectives, and challenges. They may face discrimination, stigma, and prejudice in various aspects of life, but it's essential to support and affirm their identities and rights, promoting inclusivity and understanding for all.

There's this idea in American politics that transgender people are a new phenomenon. They often think that transgender people are following a fad, or that they're making a political statement. The reality is that the history of transgender people is complex and spans across various cultures and civilizations. It's essential to recognize that the concept of gender identity and transgender experiences have been understood and accepted differently throughout history. Below, I summarize some key moments and developments in the history of transgender people:

Ancient Civilizations: Many ancient cultures, such as the Sumerians, Egyptians, Greeks, and Romans, had different understandings of gender roles and expressions. Some historical texts and artworks depict individuals who may have had non-conforming gender identities or who engaged in cross-dressing.

Indigenous Cultures: Several indigenous cultures worldwide have long recognized and embraced gender diversity. Some Native American tribes, for example, have "Two-Spirit" traditions, which honor individuals embodying both masculine and feminine qualities.

The Hijra Community: *The Hijra community in South Asia, including India, Bangladesh, and Pakistan, has existed for centuries. Hijras are often considered a distinct gender category and have a cultural and religious significance. They have historically performed roles as religious leaders, entertainers, and guardians of women's spaces.*

Edo Period in Japan: *During the Edo period (1603-1868) in Japan, "wakashu" was a term used to describe young boys who dressed in feminine clothing and were sometimes involved in relationships with older men. "Onnagata" were male actors who specialized in playing female roles in traditional Kabuki theater.*

Transgender and gender non-conforming people are a real and vital part of human history. We've always existed, and we will always exist. To say that it's a trend is simply incorrect.

Part Two: The Importance
of Self-Acceptance

The journey to accepting oneself as a transgender man can be long and arduous. Many go through phases of denial and self-hatred. I, too, tried to deny the fact that I was transgender for years. When you hide, though, it doesn't go away. Understand that it's OK to be transgender, and it's OK to feel the way you feel.

Accepting oneself as a transgender man is a significant step in the journey of self-discovery and self-acceptance. It can be a challenging process, but with patience, self-compassion, and support, you can embrace your authentic identity. Here are some steps to help you along the way:

Acknowledge and Validate Your Feelings: *Recognize and accept the feelings you have about your gender identity. It's normal to experience a range of emotions, including confusion, fear, excitement, or relief. Allow yourself to feel without judgment.*

Educate Yourself: *If you're reading this guide, you've already taken the first step! Learn about transgender experiences, gender identity, and the diverse journeys of other transgender individuals. Education can provide you with a broader understanding and a sense of community.*

Seek Support: *If you're comfortable, reach out to friends, family, or support groups who can offer understanding and encouragement. Connecting with others who have similar experiences can be invaluable.*

Professional Guidance: *Consider seeking support from a therapist or counselor experienced in transgender issues. A mental health professional can provide a safe space to explore your feelings and offer guidance.*

Journaling: Write down your thoughts and feelings in a journal. This can help you process your emotions, gain insights into your identity, and track your progress.

Practice Self-Compassion: Be kind to yourself throughout this journey. Understand that it's okay to take time to explore your identity and that self-acceptance is a process.

Focus on Positivity: Surround yourself with supportive and affirming influences. Limit exposure to negative or unsupportive environments when possible.

Celebrate Small Victories: Acknowledge and celebrate every step you take towards self-acceptance. Even small progress is worth celebrating.

Be Patient: Remember that self-acceptance is a journey and may take time. Be patient with yourself as you navigate this process.

Above all, remember that you are valid and deserving of love and acceptance. Embrace your journey as a transgender man with compassion and openness, and know that you have the strength to grow and thrive as your authentic self.

CHAPTER TWO:
COMING OUT

Part One: Finding the Right Time and Place

Coming out as transgender is a deeply personal decision, and choosing the right time and place is crucial to ensure your comfort and safety. Here are some considerations to help you determine the best time and place to come out:

Self-Reflection: Take time to reflect on your own feelings and readiness. Ensure you have a good understanding of your gender identity and are prepared for possible reactions from others. Expect a lot of questions.

Support Network: Consider the people you trust and feel closest to. Identify supportive friends, family members, or allies who are likely to be understanding and accepting. Come out to those people first, and as you grow more confident, you can come out to the world.

Safety: Prioritize your safety above all else. If you believe coming out may put you in a dangerous situation, it might be better to wait until you are in a safer environment.

Emotional Preparedness: Be emotionally prepared for a range of reactions. Some people may react positively, while others may need time to process the information. Understand that someone's initial reaction isn't a guarantee as to whether or not they'll support you. The people you are coming out to may be emotional and act irrationally. This doesn't mean they won't end up supporting you. Give people the chance to come around.

Privacy: Choose a private and comfortable setting where you can have an open and uninterrupted conversation. This can create a safe space for both you and the person you are coming out to.

Avoid Stressful Times: Try to avoid coming out during

particularly stressful or emotionally charged periods, such as holidays or family events, to ensure that the focus remains on the conversation.

One-on-One vs. Group Settings: Decide whether you prefer to come out to individuals one-on-one or in a group setting. Some people may find it easier to have individual conversations, while others might prefer a group setting for support.

Timing: Trust your intuition about when the time feels right. There may never be a perfect moment, but try to choose a time when you feel most at ease and emotionally stable. Remember — coming out is the next step to your new life!

Provide Resources: Have resources available, such as articles, books, or websites, that can help educate others about transgender experiences and address any questions they may have. There are plenty of YouTube videos nowadays that explain the transgender experience well.

Be Patient: Remember that people may need time to process the information. Be patient with their reactions and give them space if needed. It may hurt, and it may not be fair, but life isn't fair. If you want to keep your loved ones around you, allow them that time and space to process (if they so desire).

Acceptance and Rejection: Be prepared for both positive and negative reactions. While you hope for acceptance, it's important to understand that some people may not respond as you wish initially. Hope for the best, prepare for the worst. This is where the safety aspect comes into play again.

Practice: Consider rehearsing what you want to say before coming out. This can help you feel more confident during the actual conversation. You could also write a letter and have "the conversation" later on.

Ultimately, there is no universal "right" time and place to

come out as transgender. Trust your instincts, prioritize your safety, and surround yourself with supportive individuals who will embrace and accept you for who you are.

Part Two: Dealing with Negative Reactions

Unfortunately, you'll come across some non-accepting people in your lifetime. Dealing with negative reactions after coming out as transgender can be challenging, but with resilience and self-care, you can navigate these situations with strength and grace. Here are some strategies to help you cope:

Stay True to Yourself: Remember that your gender identity is valid and deserving of respect. Stay grounded in your understanding of who you are, even if others struggle to comprehend or accept it.

Seek Supportive Spaces: Surround yourself with supportive friends, family members, or members of the LGBTQ+ community who understand and embrace your identity. Seek out support groups or online forums where you can connect with others who have experienced similar challenges.

Set Boundaries: Establish clear boundaries with those who react negatively. You have the right to be treated with respect and dignity. If someone's reactions become hurtful or harmful, it may be necessary to limit your interactions with them for your emotional well-being.

Educate and Advocate: If you feel comfortable, take the opportunity to educate others about transgender experiences and address any misconceptions they may have. Advocating for your identity and sharing your journey can help foster understanding and empathy.

Seek Professional Support: Consider talking to a therapist or counselor who specializes in LGBTQ+ issues. A mental health professional can provide a safe space for you to process your emotions and provide coping strategies.

Embrace Positive Outcomes: Focus on the positive reactions and support you receive. Acknowledge the people who accept and celebrate your identity, as their acceptance can be a powerful source of strength during difficult times.

Practice Self-Care: Engage in self-care activities that help you relax and recharge. Whether it's spending time with supportive friends, practicing mindfulness, or engaging in hobbies, taking care of yourself is essential during challenging moments.

Seek Legal Advice if Needed: In cases where negative reactions lead to discrimination or harassment, consider seeking legal advice from organizations specializing in LGBTQ+ rights.

Focus on Your Journey: Remember that your transition and self-acceptance are personal journeys. You don't need to prove anything to anyone but yourself. Embrace the progress you've made and continue moving forward at your own pace.

Be Patient: You'll notice this point being repeated a lot. Changing deeply ingrained beliefs and attitudes takes time for some people. Be patient with those who may be struggling to understand or accept your identity. Their reactions may evolve with time and education.

Remember that you are not alone, and it's okay to ask for help when needed. Surround yourself with a network of support, practice self-compassion, and prioritize your well-being as you navigate negative reactions and continue on your path of self-discovery and authenticity.

CHAPTER THREE: GENDER DYSPHORIA

Part One: Understanding Dysphoria

Gender dysphoria is a term used to describe the distress or discomfort that some individuals may experience when their gender identity differs from the sex they were assigned at birth. It is important to note that not all transgender individuals experience gender dysphoria, and gender dysphoria is not a requirement for being transgender.

Gender identity refers to a person's deeply felt understanding of their own gender, which can be male, female, both, neither, or something else entirely. In contrast, sex assigned at birth is based on physical characteristics such as genitalia and chromosomes.

Gender dysphoria can manifest in various ways and can be different for each individual. Common experiences of gender dysphoria may include:

Body Dysphoria: Feeling discomfort or distress about one's physical body, particularly the primary and secondary sex characteristics that do not align with their gender identity. For example, a transgender woman may experience body dysphoria if she has facial hair or a deep voice.

Social Dysphoria: *Feeling distressed in social situations where one's gender identity is not recognized or respected. This can include being misgendered, using incorrect pronouns, or being treated as the sex assigned at birth.*

Emotional Distress: *Feeling anxious, depressed, or disconnected due to the incongruence between one's gender identity and the sex assigned at birth.*

Desire for Gender Affirmation: *Experiencing a strong desire to have one's gender identity acknowledged, affirmed, and respected by oneself and others.*

It's important to recognize that gender dysphoria is not a mental illness itself, but rather a condition that arises from the incongruence between one's gender identity and assigned sex. However, if untreated or unaddressed, gender dysphoria can lead to emotional distress and mental health challenges.

Treatment for gender dysphoria may involve social, medical, or psychological interventions. Social support, such as using the preferred name and pronouns, and wearing clothing that aligns with one's gender identity, can be affirming and helpful. Many transgender men will also wear a binder to flatten their chests. Medical interventions, such as hormone therapy or surgeries, may be pursued to alleviate body dysphoria. Psychological support, including counseling or therapy, can assist in navigating gender identity and related challenges.

Seeking professional support and connecting with the transgender community can be valuable for individuals experiencing gender dysphoria. Additionally, providing understanding, acceptance, and respect to transgender individuals can play a significant role in reducing the distress associated with gender dysphoria.

Part Two: Coping Skills
and Self-Compassion

Dealing with gender dysphoria can be a challenging and individualized process for transgender men. While it may not be possible to eliminate gender dysphoria entirely, there are several strategies that can help manage and cope with the distress it may cause. Here are some approaches that may be helpful:

Seek Professional Support: Consider working with a therapist or counselor who specializes in transgender issues and gender dysphoria. They can provide a safe and supportive space to discuss your feelings, explore coping strategies, and address any challenges you may be facing.

Social Transition: Social transition involves expressing your gender identity in your daily life, such as using your preferred name and pronouns, and wearing clothing that aligns with your gender identity. This can help alleviate some aspects of gender dysphoria related to social recognition and acceptance.

Medical Interventions: For some transgender men, medical interventions like hormone therapy (testosterone) or gender-affirming surgeries may be options to alleviate body dysphoria. These decisions are personal and should be discussed with healthcare professionals experienced in transgender care.

Connect with the Transgender Community: Engaging with the transgender community can provide support, understanding, and validation. Joining support groups or participating in online forums can be a way to connect with others who share similar experiences.

Practice Self-Care: Engage in self-care activities that promote overall well-being and help reduce stress. This can include activities such as exercise, mindfulness practices, creative hobbies, or spending time with supportive friends and loved ones.

__Educate Yourself:__ Learning more about gender dysphoria, transgender experiences, and strategies for coping can empower you to navigate your journey with more confidence and understanding.

__Set Realistic Goals:__ Recognize that gender transition is a process, and it may take time to fully address gender dysphoria. Set small, achievable goals to work towards and celebrate each step of progress.

__Challenge Negative Thoughts:__ Practice challenging negative or critical thoughts about yourself and your gender identity. Remind yourself that your identity is valid and deserving of acceptance and respect.

__Use Positive Affirmations:__ Incorporate positive affirmations into your daily routine to reinforce self-acceptance and build confidence in your gender identity.

__Reach Out for Support:__ Don't hesitate to reach out to friends, family, or other supportive individuals in your life. Having a strong support network can make a significant difference in managing gender dysphoria.

Remember that everyone's journey with gender dysphoria is unique, and what works for one person may not work for another. It's essential to prioritize your well-being and find strategies that resonate with you personally. If you're struggling to cope with gender dysphoria, seeking professional help is always a valuable option. You don't have to navigate this journey alone, and there are resources available to support you along the way.

CHAPTER FOUR: UNDERSTANDING HORMONE THERAPY AND MEDICAL TRANSITION

Part One: Accessing Healthcare and Professional Support

Accessing competent and affirming healthcare is a crucial aspect of the well-being and overall quality of life for transgender men. Unfortunately, healthcare disparities and challenges in understanding transgender-specific needs have been persistent. In this chapter, we will explore the importance of finding healthcare providers who are knowledgeable about transgender healthcare, the process of accessing hormone therapy, and considerations for gender-affirming surgeries.

Transgender men often face unique healthcare needs related to gender-affirming care, hormone therapy, mental health, and sexual health. To ensure comprehensive and supportive care, it is essential to seek healthcare providers who are knowledgeable and affirming of transgender experiences.

Ask for Recommendations: Reach out to the transgender community, support groups, or LGBTQ+ organizations for recommendations of healthcare providers who have experience in transgender healthcare.

Check Online Directories: Some online directories or resources list healthcare providers who have expressed their expertise in providing transgender healthcare. Look for providers who mention transgender care in their profiles or practice descriptions.

Interview Potential Providers: Schedule consultations with potential healthcare providers to ask about their experience, knowledge, and approach to transgender healthcare. Find someone who makes you feel respected and heard. Hormone therapy is a common aspect of gender-affirming care for transgender men, as it helps align physical characteristics with gender identity. However, starting hormone therapy requires careful consideration and guidance from a knowledgeable healthcare provider.

Mental Health Evaluation: Many healthcare providers will require a mental health evaluation before starting hormone therapy to ensure that you are emotionally prepared for the physical and emotional changes that may occur.

Informed Consent Model: Some healthcare providers follow the informed consent model, which allows eligible individuals to start hormone therapy without a mental health evaluation. Instead, they are provided with comprehensive information about the effects and potential risks of hormone therapy.

Monitoring and Adjustments: Regular follow-up appointments are essential to monitor your progress, assess any side effects, and make necessary adjustments to your hormone regimen to achieve the desired outcomes.

Gender-affirming surgeries, such as mastectomy (top surgery) or genital reconstruction (bottom surgery), are significant steps for some transgender men in aligning their bodies with their gender identity.

Consultation and Evaluation: To explore the possibility of gender-affirming surgeries, schedule consultations with experienced surgeons. They will assess your physical health, mental readiness, and discuss the surgical procedures and potential outcomes.

Preparing for Surgery: If you decide to proceed with gender-affirming surgery, your healthcare provider will guide you through pre-surgical preparations, including necessary medical evaluations and instructions for pre-surgery care.

Post-Surgical Care: After surgery, follow your surgeon's post-operative instructions carefully to ensure proper healing and *recovery. Attend follow-up appointments for ongoing evaluation and support.*

Unfortunately, transgender individuals may encounter barriers to accessing healthcare, such as discrimination, lack of knowledge among healthcare providers, or financial limitations.

Advocate for Yourself: *Know your rights as a patient and advocate for respectful and affirming care. Don't hesitate to speak up if you experience discrimination or encounter barriers to accessing appropriate healthcare.*

Seek Financial Assistance: *Explore financial assistance programs, insurance coverage options, or nonprofit organizations that support transgender individuals' access to healthcare.*

Overall, accessing healthcare and professional support is a critical aspect of the transgender experience. Finding knowledgeable and affirming healthcare providers, navigating hormone therapy and gender-affirming surgeries, and prioritizing mental health support are essential steps in ensuring a positive and empowering transition journey for transgender men. Remember that you deserve respectful and competent care, and there are resources and support available to help you navigate this process.

Part Two: HRT 101

Taking testosterone, also known as hormone replacement therapy (HRT), is a significant step for many transgender men in their gender affirmation journey. This comprehensive guide aims to provide essential information and considerations for individuals seeking to begin testosterone therapy. Before starting HRT, it's crucial to consult a knowledgeable healthcare provider experienced in transgender healthcare to ensure a safe and effective transition process.

First off, what exactly is testosterone? Testosterone is a hormone that belongs to a class of hormones known as androgens. It is the primary male sex hormone and plays a vital role in the development and maintenance of male sexual characteristics. Testosterone is produced in the testes in biological males and in smaller amounts in the ovaries and adrenal glands in biological females.

Testosterone is responsible for sexual development. During puberty, testosterone stimulates the development of primary sexual characteristics, such as the growth of the testes and the production of sperm. It also contributes to the development of secondary sexual characteristics, such as the deepening of the voice, growth of facial and body hair, and increased muscle mass.

In transgender healthcare, testosterone is often prescribed to transgender men as hormone replacement therapy (HRT) to align their physical characteristics with their gender identity. This therapy aims to induce the development of male secondary sexual characteristics, helping transgender men feel more comfortable in their bodies and achieve a gender-affirming appearance. Testosterone therapy for transgender men is typically administered through injections, gels, patches, or pellets under the guidance of healthcare professionals experienced in transgender healthcare.

So, having said all of that, let's move on to administration methods:

Intramuscular Injections: *Testosterone can be administered via intramuscular injections. Injections are typically given into the muscle, such as the glutes or thighs, and are usually done weekly or every few weeks, depending on the prescribed dosage. Intramuscular injections provide a steady release of testosterone and are a popular choice for many transgender men.*

Subcutaneous Injections: *Subcutaneous injections are similar to intramuscular injections but involve injecting the testosterone just beneath the skin instead of into the muscle. The injections are typically administered in the abdomen or thigh. Subcutaneous injections may be less painful and may be preferred by some individuals. The needle is much shorter.*

Topical Gels: *Testosterone gels are applied to the skin and absorbed through the skin into the bloodstream. They are usually applied daily to the upper arms, shoulders, or abdomen. Gels offer a convenient and discreet method of administration, but caution should be taken to prevent transfer to others, especially children and pregnant individuals.*

Transdermal Patches: *Testosterone patches are worn on the skin, usually on the abdomen, back, or upper arms. They release a continuous and steady dose of testosterone through the skin. Patches are typically changed once a day or every few days, depending on the brand and dosage. They are not as popular as injections or gel.*

Buccal Patches or Tablets: *Buccal patches or tablets are placed against the inner cheek and allowed to dissolve. The testosterone is absorbed through the mucous membranes in the* *mouth. This method offers an alternative to injections and may be preferred by some individuals.*

Testosterone Pellets: Testosterone pellets are small implants placed under the skin, usually in the buttocks or abdomen, during a minor surgical procedure.

These pellets release a consistent dose of testosterone over several months, eliminating the need for frequent administration.

It's essential for transgender men to work closely with an experienced healthcare provider to determine the most suitable method of testosterone administration based on individual health needs, lifestyle, and preferences. Regular monitoring of hormone levels and overall health is essential throughout the course of testosterone therapy to ensure safe and effective results.

Now, what are the side effects of testosterone? The timeline for testosterone effects in transgender men can vary widely from person to person. Hormone therapy is a gradual process, and individual responses to testosterone can be influenced by factors such as age, genetics, dosage, and overall health. It's important to remember that everyone's journey is unique, and not all individuals will experience the same changes at the same rate. The following timeline provides a general overview of the typical changes that transgender men may experience while undergoing testosterone therapy:

0 to 3 Months:
- *Increased Energy: Some individuals may notice an increase in energy levels and overall well-being shortly after starting testosterone.*
- *Skin Changes: The skin may become oilier, and acne may develop or worsen.*

- *Body Fat Redistribution: Fat may begin to redistribute, typically leading to a decrease in subcutaneous fat in the hips and thighs and an increase in abdominal fat.*
- *Clitoral Growth: The clitoris may begin to enlarge slightly due to increased blood flow.*
- *Libido Changes: Some individuals may experience an increase in sex drive (libido).*

3 to 6 Months:

- *Body Hair Growth: Increased hair growth, particularly on the face, chest, and abdomen, may become more noticeable.*
- *Voice Changes: The voice may start to lower, and vocal resonance may shift towards a more masculine tone.*
- *Muscle Mass Increase: Some individuals may notice an increase in muscle mass and strength, particularly with regular exercise and strength training.*

6 to 12 Months:
- *Facial Hair Growth: Facial hair may continue to thicken and become more prominent, although the growth pattern varies among individuals.*
- *Scalp & Hair Changes: Some individuals may experience mild hairline recession or a change in hair texture and thickness.*
- *Body Shape Changes: The body may continue to masculinize, with a reduction in hip width and an increase in shoulder width.*

1 to 2 Years:
- *Voice Stabilization: The voice typically stabilizes, with fewer noticeable changes in pitch.*

- *Facial and Body Hair Development: Facial hair and body hair may continue to thicken and fill in.*
- *Changes in Body Odor: Body odor may become more musky or masculine.*

Beyond 2 Years:

- *Finalizing Changes: Most physical changes resulting from testosterone therapy are expected to stabilize by this point.*
- *Continuation of Hair Growth: Facial and body hair may continue to develop over time.*
- *Muscle Development: Ongoing exercise and strength training can lead to continued muscle development.*

It's important to note that not all individuals will experience every change listed, and some changes may occur earlier or later than the specified timeline. Additionally, some changes, such as facial hair growth and voice changes, may continue to develop over several years. Regular monitoring by a qualified healthcare provider is essential throughout the process to ensure safe and effective hormone therapy and to address any concerns or complications that may arise.

Part Three: Potential Risks

Taking testosterone as a transgender man (hormone replacement therapy, or HRT) can lead to desired physical changes and align one's appearance with their gender identity. However, like any medical treatment, testosterone therapy carries certain risks and potential side effects. It's crucial to work closely with a qualified healthcare provider experienced in transgender healthcare to manage these risks and ensure safe and effective hormone therapy. Some of the risks of taking testosterone as a transgender man include:

- Increased Blood Pressure: Testosterone can cause a slight increase in blood pressure, which may be a concern for individuals with pre-existing cardiovascular conditions.

- Changes in Cholesterol Levels: Testosterone therapy can impact cholesterol levels, potentially leading to increases in "bad" LDL cholesterol.

- Liver Health: Testosterone is metabolized in the liver, and long-term use may cause mild changes in liver function in some individuals. Regular monitoring of liver health is important.

- Fertility: Testosterone therapy often leads to a cessation of menstrual cycles (amenorrhea) in transgender men. However, it's essential to understand that fertility may not be entirely suppressed, and pregnancy remains possible if precautions are not taken. Prolonged testosterone use can lead to reduced fertility or permanent infertility. If preserving fertility is a priority, discuss fertility preservation options with your healthcare provider before starting HRT.

- Mood Swings: Some individuals may experience mood swings or changes in emotional responses as their hormone levels fluctuate.

- Emotional Changes: Testosterone can influence emotions, energy levels, and assertiveness, though the effects are highly individualized.

- Increased Oil Production: Testosterone can stimulate oil production, leading to acne or exacerbating existing acne in some individuals.

- Male Pattern Baldness: Individuals with a genetic predisposition for male pattern baldness may experience accelerated hair loss while on testosterone therapy.

- Body Odor: Testosterone can lead to changes in body odor, becoming more musky or masculine.

Like with testosterone's benefits, it's important to note that not all transgender men will experience all of these risks or side effects. The effects of testosterone therapy can vary widely among individuals. Regular monitoring and open communication with a healthcare provider are essential to manage any potential risks and ensure the overall safety and effectiveness of hormone therapy. If any concerning side effects arise, discuss them with your healthcare provider promptly.

CHAPTER FIVE: EMBRACING YOUR AUTHENTIC STYLE

Part One: Exploring Clothing and Fashion Choices

Exploring clothing and fashion choices as a transgender man can be a liberating and empowering journey. Here are some steps and tips to help you on your path:

Self-Discovery: Take some time to understand your personal style preferences, what makes you feel comfortable and confident, and how you want to express your identity through clothing. Explore different styles, colors, and patterns to find what resonates with you.

Role Models and Inspiration: Look for role models and individuals who share your gender identity and have a fashion sense that you admire. Follow fashion influencers, celebrities, or simply people in your community whose style aligns with your taste.

Online Research: Utilize the internet to research and explore various styles, brands, and clothing options that cater to your body type and gender identity. There are many online communities and resources for transgender men, where you can find fashion tips and advice.

Dress for Your Body Shape: Understanding your body shape can help you choose clothes that flatter your figure and make you feel more comfortable. Embrace clothing that emphasizes your best features and allows you to move freely.

Thrifting and Experimenting: Thrift stores can be a treasure trove for finding unique and affordable clothing options. Don't be afraid to experiment with different pieces and styles to see what works for you.

Seek Supportive Spaces: If you feel comfortable, join local or online LGBTQ+ support groups where you can share experiences, ideas, *and tips on fashion and style.*

***Tailoring:** Sometimes, off-the-rack clothing may not fit perfectly, so consider finding a tailor who can help adjust clothes to fit your body shape better. Customizing clothes can make a significant difference in how you feel about your appearance.*

***Mix and Match:** Don't feel restricted by traditional gender norms in fashion. Feel free to mix and match clothing items and styles from different sections of the store. Play with androgynous or gender-neutral looks if that suits your taste.*

***Stay True to Yourself:** Remember that fashion is a form of self-expression, so don't feel pressured to conform to anyone else's expectations. Choose clothing that resonates with your authentic self and makes you feel confident and happy.*

***Take Your Time:** Building a wardrobe that aligns with your identity may take time, and that's okay. Fashion and style are fluid and can evolve over time, so enjoy the process of exploring and discovering what works best for you.*

Lastly, remember that there is no one "right" way to be a transgender man, and your clothing choices are entirely your own. Embrace your unique identity, and have fun exploring the world of fashion on your terms!

Part Two: Choosing a Masculine Hairstyle

Choosing a masculine hairstyle that suits you as a transgender man is a personal decision that should be based on your preferences, facial features, hair texture, and lifestyle. Here are some steps to help you find a masculine hairstyle that feels right for you:

Research and Gather Inspiration: Start by looking at images of different masculine hairstyles online or in magazines. Consider the hairstyles of celebrities or individuals whose facial features are similar to yours. This will give you a sense of what styles you like and what might work well for you.

Consider Your Hair Texture: Take into account your natural hair texture when choosing a hairstyle. Some styles may work better with straight hair, while others are more suitable for curly or wavy hair. If you're unsure, consult with a hairstylist who can advise you on the best options for your hair type.

Facial Features: Consider your facial features and head shape when choosing a hairstyle. Certain cuts can complement and enhance your features. For example, shorter hairstyles can accentuate the jawline and cheekbones.

Lifestyle and Maintenance: Think about your lifestyle and how much time you are willing to invest in styling and maintaining your hair. Some styles require more upkeep, while others are more low-maintenance.

Consult with a Hairstylist: Schedule an appointment with a hairstylist who is experienced with men's haircuts and has an understanding of gender-affirming hairstyles. Discuss your preferences, lifestyle, and any concerns you may have. A skilled hairstylist can offer valuable insights and help you find a haircut that aligns with your identity.

Experiment with Length: *If you're uncertain about a dramatic change, consider starting with a slightly shorter version of a potential hairstyle and gradually go shorter if you feel comfortable.*

Embrace Androgyny if Desired: *If you prefer a more androgynous look, consider hairstyles that blend elements of both masculine and feminine styles. These styles can be a unique way to express your identity.*

Confidence is Key: *Ultimately, the most important factor in choosing a masculine hairstyle is how it makes you feel. Confidence in your appearance can be a powerful aspect of self-expression, so choose a style that resonates with your sense of self.*

Be Patient: *Finding the perfect hairstyle might take some time and experimentation. Don't be afraid to try different styles until you discover the one that truly suits you.*

Remember, there is no one "right" masculine hairstyle for every transgender man. Embrace your individuality and choose a hairstyle that helps you feel authentic and comfortable in your own skin.

Part Three: Personal Grooming and Body Confidence

Grooming as a transgender man can be a personal and affirming experience. Here are some grooming tips to help you feel confident and comfortable in your body:

Haircare: *Choose a hairstyle that aligns with your gender identity and is easy to maintain. Regular haircuts can help keep your hair looking fresh and well-groomed. Use hair products suitable for your hair type and style, such as shampoo, conditioner, and styling products.*

Facial Hair: *If you have facial hair that you wish to keep, consider grooming it regularly to maintain a clean and neat appearance. Shaving, trimming, or shaping your facial hair can help you achieve the desired look.*

Skincare: *Develop a skincare routine that suits your skin type. Cleansing, moisturizing, and using sunscreen can promote healthy skin and reduce the chances of skin issues.*

Body Hair: *Decide on your comfort level with body hair. Some transgender men prefer to remove body hair through shaving, waxing, or other methods, while others choose to keep it as is. The decision is entirely up to you.*

Nail Care: *Keep your nails clean and trimmed. If you like, you can explore nail grooming, such as nail filing and buffing, or even experimenting with nail polish if that aligns with your style.*

Body Odor: *Use deodorant or antiperspirant to manage body odor. Find a scent or product that you enjoy and works well for your body.*

Clothing and Style: *Grooming extends to your clothing and personal style. Choose clothes that match your gender identity and make you feel confident and comfortable.*

Bathing and Hygiene: Maintain good personal hygiene by showering regularly and practicing proper dental care. Brush your teeth at least twice a day and floss regularly.

Beard Care (if applicable): If you have facial hair, invest in beard care products like beard oil or balm to keep your beard healthy and well-groomed.

Seek Professional Help: If you're unsure about grooming techniques or products, consider seeking help from professionals. Barbers, stylists, and estheticians can provide guidance tailored to your specific needs.

Be Patient and Compassionate: Grooming routines and habits may take time to develop. Be patient with yourself and show self-compassion as you explore what works best for you.

Remember that grooming is a personal choice, and there is no one-size-fits-all approach. Prioritize what feels right and comfortable for you as you express your gender identity through grooming practices. If you have any specific questions or concerns about grooming techniques or products, don't hesitate to reach out to supportive communities or professionals who understand the needs of transgender individuals.

Being confident in your body as a transgender man is a journey that involves self-acceptance, self-love, and understanding. Here are some tips to help you build body confidence:

Self-Reflection: Take time to understand and appreciate your body. Focus on the positive aspects of your physical self and celebrate what makes you unique.

Surround Yourself with Supportive People: Build a support

network of friends, family, or community members who affirm and validate your gender identity. Positive and understanding relationships can boost your self-confidence.

Seek Professional Support: If you're struggling with body image issues or self-acceptance, consider speaking to a therapist or counselor who specializes in gender identity and body positivity. Professional guidance can be immensely beneficial.

Positive Affirmations: Practice positive self-talk. Replace negative thoughts with affirmations that reinforce your self-worth and body positivity.

Focus on Strengths and Abilities: Shift your focus from appearance alone to what your body can do. Celebrate your strengths, skills, and talents, as they are not tied to any specific body image.

Set Realistic Goals: Set achievable goals related to fitness, health, or personal growth. Working towards and reaching these goals can enhance body confidence.

Dress in a Way that Affirms Your Identity: Wear clothes that make you feel comfortable and confident in your gender identity. Dressing in a way that aligns with who you are can positively impact your self-perception.

Practice Self-Care: Engage in self-care activities that nurture your mind, body, and soul. Whether it's meditation, exercise, reading, or hobbies, taking care of yourself holistically can improve body confidence.

Challenge Social Norms and Stereotypes: Recognize that societal standards of beauty and masculinity are often unrealistic and limited. Embrace diversity and understand that there is no one "right" way to be a transgender man.

Limit Comparisons: Avoid comparing yourself to others, as it can negatively impact your self-esteem. Focus on your own progress and growth.

Embrace Gratitude: Cultivate gratitude for the things your body allows you to experience and enjoy. Gratitude can shift your perspective and lead to greater body acceptance.

Educate Others: If you feel comfortable, educate others about transgender experiences and the importance of body acceptance and respect for all individuals.

Body confidence is a process, and it's normal to have ups and downs. Be patient with yourself and allow room for growth and self-discovery. Every step you take towards accepting and loving your body brings you closer to genuine confidence and self-empowerment as a transgender man.

CHAPTER SIX:
BUILDING A
SUPPORTIVE
COMMUNITY

Part One: Connecting with Other Transgender Men

Connecting with other transgender men can be a valuable and supportive experience. Here are some ways to find and connect with the transgender community:

LGBTQ+ Support Groups: Look for LGBTQ+ support groups or organizations in your local community. Many areas have transgender-specific groups where you can meet and connect with other transgender men.

Online Forums and Social Media: There are numerous online forums, social media groups, and communities specifically dedicated to transgender individuals. Platforms like Reddit, Facebook, and Twitter have transgender-specific groups where you can interact and share experiences with others.

Attend LGBTQ+ Events: Check for LGBTQ+ events, workshops, conferences, or pride celebrations in your area. These gatherings provide opportunities to meet and connect with other transgender men and the broader LGBTQ+ community.

Transgender Health Clinics: Many transgender health clinics or LGBTQ+-friendly medical centers host support groups or community events for transgender individuals. Inquire if there are any such programs available in your area.

Transgender Meetups: Search for transgender-specific meetups in your region using websites like Meetup.com. These events offer casual and social settings to meet other transgender individuals.

Online Networking: Utilize social media platforms like LinkedIn to network with other transgender professionals or individuals who share your interests.

Volunteer for LGBTQ+ Causes: Get involved with LGBTQ

+ *organizations or causes as a volunteer. This not only helps you connect with others but also contributes to the community.*

Attend Workshops or Conferences: *Attend workshops or conferences that focus on transgender-related topics. These events can provide networking opportunities and educational experiences.*

Reach Out to Local LGBTQ+ Centers: *Check if there are any LGBTQ+ centers or organizations in your area that host support groups or social events for transgender individuals.*

Engage in Online Chats and Discussions: *Participate in online chats and discussions on transgender-related topics. Engaging in these conversations can help you connect with like-minded individuals.*

When connecting with other transgender men, remember to approach interactions with respect and an open mind. Share your experiences and listen to the stories of others. Building a network of supportive individuals can provide a sense of belonging and understanding as you navigate your journey as a transgender man.

Part Two: Nurturing Relationships and Allies

Nurturing relationships and allies as a transgender man is essential for building a strong support system and fostering understanding and acceptance. Here are some tips to help you in this process:

Be Open and Honest: *Share your experiences and feelings openly with your friends, family, and potential allies. Honest communication can lead to deeper connections and a better understanding of your journey.*

Educate and Advocate: *Provide information about transgender issues and experiences to your allies. Education can help dispel misconceptions and create a more inclusive and empathetic environment.*

Set Boundaries: *Establish boundaries in your relationships to ensure that you are respected and supported. Communicate your needs and limits to those around you.*

Find Common Interests: *Cultivate relationships based on shared interests and hobbies. Common activities can strengthen connections and foster a sense of camaraderie.*

Practice Active Listening: *Show genuine interest in the thoughts and feelings of your friends and allies. Active listening fosters trust and encourages open dialogue.*

Express Gratitude: *Let your allies know that you appreciate their support and understanding. A simple thank-you can go a long way in nurturing relationships.*

Be Patient and Understanding: Understand that not everyone may immediately grasp transgender issues or the challenges you face. Be patient and willing to answer questions or offer guidance.

Engage in Mutual Support: *Offer support and*

encouragement to your allies when they need it. Building reciprocal relationships strengthens bonds and fosters trust.

***Share Positive Experiences:** Celebrate your successes and positive experiences with your allies. Sharing these moments can create a more uplifting and supportive environment.*

***Attend LGBTQ+ Events Together:** Participate in LGBTQ+ events, workshops, or pride celebrations with your allies. These shared experiences can deepen connections and foster a sense of community.*

Be Mindful of Language: Encourage the use of inclusive language that respects your gender identity and pronouns. Correcting misunderstandings or misgendering in a patient and understanding manner can help educate others.

***Engage in Social Media Activism:** Share educational content and advocate for transgender rights and issues on social media. Your allies may learn from your posts and be inspired to support the cause.*

***Celebrate Allyship:** Acknowledge and appreciate the efforts of your allies to support and understand you. Allies who feel valued and recognized are more likely to continue supporting you.*

Remember that nurturing relationships and allies is an ongoing process. Building strong connections requires time, effort, and patience. Surrounding yourself with understanding and supportive individuals can greatly enhance your well-being and sense of belonging as a transgender man.

CHAPTER SIX:
LEGAL RIGHTS AND
DOCUMENTATION

Part One: Name and Gender Marker Changes

Getting your legal name changed as a transgender man involves a series of steps, and the process may vary depending on the country or state you reside in. Here's a general outline of the steps involved in the name change process:

Research the Requirements: Begin by researching the specific name change requirements in your country and state or province. Check the laws, regulations, and procedures related to name changes for transgender individuals.

Gather Necessary Documents: Typically, you will need identification documents, such as your birth certificate, passport, driver's license, and Social Security card. Some jurisdictions might also require additional documentation, like a court order or gender marker change.

Choose a New Name: Decide on the new legal name you want to use. Ensure that the name adheres to the legal requirements and is not prohibited or offensive in your jurisdiction.

Consult with an Attorney (Optional): While it's not always necessary, consulting with an attorney who specializes in LGBTQ + legal matters can be helpful, especially if you encounter any challenges during the process.

File the Name Change Petition: Obtain the necessary forms from the appropriate government office (usually the courthouse or local civil registrar's office) and complete the name change petition. You might need to pay a filing fee.

Affidavit or Declaration: In some places, you may need to submit an affidavit or declaration stating that you are changing your name for reasons other than fraud or evasion of legal obligations.

Court Hearing (if required): Depending on your location, you might need to attend a court hearing to present your name change petition. The court will review your request, and if everything is in order, they will grant the name change.

Obtain a Court Order: If your name change is approved, you will receive a court order that officially changes your name.

Update Your Identification and Records: After obtaining the court order, update your identification documents, including your Social Security card, driver's license, passport, and any other legal documents that bear your previous name.

Update Other Records: Notify relevant agencies, organizations, banks, schools, and other entities about your name change to ensure all records reflect your new legal name.

It's essential to be patient throughout the process, as it may take some time to complete all the steps and update your records. Be sure to follow the specific guidelines and requirements in your jurisdiction to ensure a smooth and successful name change as a transgender man.

Getting your legal gender marker changed is also an important step in affirming your gender identity. The process varies depending on the country, state, or region you live in. Here are general steps to guide you through the process:

Research Local Laws and Requirements: Start by researching the legal gender marker change requirements in your country or state. Look for information on the government websites or consult LGBTQ+ legal resources.

Obtain Necessary Documents: You will likely need specific documents to support your gender marker change request. These may include a letter from a healthcare provider, therapist, or gender specialist confirming your gender identity. Some places may also require a court order or a notarized affidavit.

Consult with Legal Professionals (Optional): *If you're uncertain about the process or face legal challenges, consider seeking advice from a lawyer specializing in transgender legal issues. They can guide you through the process and ensure you meet all requirements.*

Complete Gender Marker Change Forms: *Obtain the necessary forms from the appropriate government office (usually the courthouse or vital records office). Fill out the forms accurately and honestly.*

Submit Required Documentation: *Attach any supporting documents, such as a letter from a healthcare professional, as required by the government office.*

Pay Any Fees: *Some places may charge fees for changing your gender marker. Be prepared to pay any required costs.*

Attend a Court Hearing (if required): *In some jurisdictions, a court hearing may be necessary to process the gender marker change request. If a hearing is required, attend and present your case.*

Receive Legal Documentation: *Once your request is approved, you'll receive legal documentation, such as a court order or amended birth certificate, reflecting your updated gender marker.*

Update Identification and Records: *Use the legal documentation to update your identification documents, such as your driver's license, passport, Social Security card, and other official records.*

Inform Other Entities: *Notify other relevant agencies, organizations, schools, banks, and healthcare providers about your gender marker change to update their records.*

Remember that the process can vary significantly based

on your location and local laws. Some jurisdictions might have more straightforward processes, while others may have stricter requirements. Be patient, follow the guidelines carefully, and seek assistance if needed to ensure a successful gender marker change.

Part Two: Understanding Anti-Discrimination Laws

As of 2021, there are several federal and state-level anti-discrimination laws in place to protect transgender Americans from discrimination. Here are some of the key federal laws and regulations that offer protections:

Title VII of the Civil Rights Act of 1964: Title VII prohibits discrimination based on sex in employment, which has been interpreted by the U.S. Supreme Court to include protections for transgender individuals. This means that employers cannot discriminate against transgender employees or job applicants based on their gender identity.

Equal Employment Opportunity Commission (EEOC) Guidance: The EEOC, the federal agency responsible for enforcing Title VII, has issued guidance clarifying that discrimination against transgender individuals is a form of sex discrimination and is prohibited.

Affordable Care Act (ACA): Section 1557 of the ACA prohibits discrimination based on sex, which includes discrimination against transgender individuals in healthcare settings. This means that healthcare providers and insurers cannot deny or limit coverage or services based on gender identity.

Housing and Urban Development (HUD) Regulations: HUD has issued regulations that prohibit discrimination based on sex, which includes discrimination against transgender individuals, in federally funded housing programs.

Title IX of the Education Amendments of 1972: Title IX prohibits sex discrimination in educational institutions that receive federal funding. Courts have ruled that this includes protections for transgender students against discrimination and harassment.

Military Service: In 2021, President Joe Biden signed an executive order reversing the ban on transgender individuals serving openly in the U.S. military, restoring protections for transgender service members.

It's important to note that legal protections can vary from state to state, and some states may have additional laws providing protections for transgender individuals against discrimination in areas such as public accommodations, education, and healthcare.

While these laws and regulations offer important protections, transgender individuals may still face discrimination in various aspects of their lives. Advocacy and education efforts continue to work towards full equality and protections for transgender Americans. If you believe you have experienced discrimination, it's essential to know your rights and seek legal advice or report the incident to the appropriate government agency.

Unfortunately, as the years have gone by, the amount of hostility towards trans people has increased tenfold. Many states have various discriminatory laws in their respective legislatures. On the other hand, though, some blue states have declared themselves as transgender sanctuaries. This means that transgender people can live there without facing discrimination from their previous state.

CHAPTER EIGHT: NAVIGATING RELATIONSHIPS AND DATING

Part One: Communicating your Transgender Identity

Although it's a bit controversial within the community, as a general rule, you should communicate to your partners that you are transgender early on. Your safety is put at risk the longer you wait, as is your relationship. If the partner reacts poorly, you wouldn't have wanted to be with them anyways.

Communicating your transgender identity to romantic and sexual partners is an important step in building trust, intimacy, and mutual understanding in a relationship. Here are some tips to help you navigate this conversation:

Choose the Right Time and Setting: *Find a comfortable and private setting where you can have an uninterrupted conversation. Choose a time when both you and your partner are relaxed and open to discussing important matters.*

Be Honest and Authentic: *Approach the conversation with honesty and authenticity. Share your transgender identity openly and sincerely, expressing your feelings and experiences.*

Educate Your Partner: *Be prepared to educate your partner about transgender issues, if necessary. Many people may not be familiar with transgender experiences, so providing information can help them better understand your journey.*

Use "I" Statements: *Share your feelings and experiences using "I" statements to avoid sounding accusatory. For example, say, "I am transgender, and it's important for me to be honest about my identity," rather than, "You need to know that I am transgender."*

Address Their Feelings: *Understand that your partner might have questions or concerns. Be patient and address their feelings with empathy and openness.*

Set Boundaries: If there are certain aspects of your identity or transition that you prefer to keep private, it's okay to set boundaries and share only what you feel comfortable disclosing at that moment.

Be Prepared for Various Reactions: People may react differently to the news, ranging from complete acceptance to confusion or uncertainty. Be prepared for various reactions, and give your partner time to process the information.

Offer Resources: Provide your partner with resources, such as websites, books, or support groups, where they can learn more about transgender experiences and get additional support.

Emphasize Trust and Communication: Reinforce the importance of trust and open communication in your relationship. Let your partner know that you value their understanding and support.

Discuss the Relationship Moving Forward: Talk about how your transgender identity may impact your relationship. Address any concerns or questions your partner may have about the future.

Advocate for Your Needs: Let your partner know how they can support you in your gender journey. Be clear about your needs and what kind of support is most helpful to you.

Give Them Space to Process: Understand that your partner may need time to process the information and come to terms with it. Be patient and allow them the space they need to do so.

At the end of the day, remember that disclosing your transgender identity is a personal decision, and you have the right to share this information at a pace that feels comfortable for you. While I can recommend that you do it early, only you know what's best for you. Building a strong foundation of open communication and understanding with your partner is essential in any relationship, and discussing your transgender identity is an important part of that process.

Part Two: Fostering Healthy and Respectful Relationships

Fostering healthy and respectful romantic relationships as a transgender man involves nurturing open communication, understanding, and mutual support. Here are some tips to help you build a positive and affirming romantic connection:

Self-Awareness: *Understand and embrace your own identity and needs as a transgender man. Being comfortable and confident in your identity can help you communicate your needs effectively to your partner.*

Open Communication: *Foster open and honest communication with your partner. Share your feelings, experiences, and concerns, and encourage your partner to do the same.*

Educate Your Partner: *If your partner is unfamiliar with transgender experiences, offer them resources and information to help them better understand your journey.*

Set Boundaries: *Clearly communicate your boundaries and expectations in the relationship. Respect each other's boundaries and create a safe space for expressing needs and concerns.*

Be Patient and Understanding: *Recognize that your partner may need time to learn and adjust to your experiences as a transgender man. Be patient and understanding during this process.*

Support Each Other: *Offer support and encouragement to each other in all aspects of life. Being each other's cheerleaders can strengthen your bond.*

Celebrate Your Identities: *Celebrate each other's individual identities and appreciate the unique qualities you both bring to the relationship.*

Advocate for Yourself: *Advocate for your needs within the* relationship. *Make sure your partner respects and supports your identity and choices.*

Empower Each Other: *Encourage each other's personal growth and self-expression. Support each other's goals and aspirations.*

Build Trust: *Trust is the foundation of a healthy relationship. Be trustworthy, and work on building trust with your partner.*

Handle Conflict Respectfully: *Disagreements are a natural part of any relationship. Handle conflicts with respect and avoid harmful or hurtful language.*

Affirm Each Other: *Offer affirmations and positive reinforcement to each other. Make sure your partner knows they are valued and loved.*

Seek Support if Needed: *If you encounter challenges in your relationship, consider seeking support from a therapist or counselor who specializes in LGBTQ+ relationships.*

Celebrate Your Love: *Celebrate your love for each other and the journey you're taking together. Create memorable experiences and cherish the moments you share.*

Remember that every relationship is unique, and communication is key. Be open to learning and growing together, and be sure to prioritize your well-being and happiness in the relationship. A healthy and respectful romantic relationship is built on a foundation of love, trust, understanding, and mutual support.

CHAPTER NINE: ADDRESSING SAFETY AND ADVOCACY

Part One: Staying Safe in Various Environments

Ensuring your safety as a transgender person involves being proactive and vigilant in various environments. While it's unfortunate that discrimination and prejudice still exist, there are steps you can take to protect yourself. Here are some safety tips:

Trust Your Instincts: Listen to your instincts and intuition. If a situation feels uncomfortable or unsafe, remove yourself from it if possible.

Be Mindful of Surroundings: Stay aware of your surroundings, especially in unfamiliar places or areas known for intolerance. Avoid walking alone at night if possible.

Share Your Location: When meeting new people or going to unfamiliar locations, consider sharing your location with a trusted friend or family member for added safety.

Educate Yourself on Local Laws: Know the laws and regulations regarding LGBTQ+ rights and protections in the places you visit or live. This knowledge can help you understand your legal rights and recourse in case of discrimination or harassment.

Build a Supportive Network: Surround yourself with friends, family, or LGBTQ+ support groups who can provide emotional support and assistance if needed.

Use Gender-Neutral Restrooms (If Desired and Available): If you feel uncomfortable using gendered restrooms, seek out gender-neutral or single-stall restrooms where available.

Avoid Revealing Personal Information: Be cautious about sharing personal information online or with strangers. Protect your privacy to prevent potential harm.

Report Discrimination: If you encounter discrimination or

harassment, consider reporting it to the appropriate authorities, whether it's at work, in public places, or online.

Be Cautious with Online Dating: If using dating apps, exercise caution and meet in public places for the first few encounters. Inform a friend or family member about your plans. Dating apps are often full of people who fetishize transgender men, and they may act as predators.

Travel in Pairs or Groups: Whenever possible, travel with a friend or in a group, as there is safety in numbers.

Stay Informed: Keep updated on LGBTQ+ events and gatherings that may offer a safe and supportive environment.

Have an Exit Plan: If you find yourself in an uncomfortable or dangerous situation, have an exit plan ready.

Know Your Rights: Familiarize yourself with your legal rights and protections as a transgender individual in different situations.

Seek Allies: Build relationships with allies who support and stand up for LGBTQ+ rights. Allies can be valuable advocates and provide a safer environment.

Remember, it's not your responsibility to tolerate discrimination or harassment. If you ever feel unsafe, reach out for help and support. Surround yourself with people who respect and value you for who you are. By being proactive and informed, you can take steps to increase your safety and well-being in various environments.

Part Two: Self-Defense and Personal Security Tips

Self-defense and personal safety are essential skills for everyone to learn. Here are some tips to help you stay safe and protect yourself:

Be Aware of Your Surroundings: *Stay alert and aware of your surroundings at all times. Avoid distractions like using your phone excessively while walking or in public spaces.*

Trust Your Instincts: *If a situation feels uncomfortable or unsafe, trust your instincts and remove yourself from it if possible.*

Avoid Isolated Areas: *When walking or jogging, stick to well-lit and populated areas. Avoid shortcuts through isolated or unfamiliar places, especially at night.*

Walk with Confidence: *Appear confident and purposeful when walking alone. Stand tall, make eye contact, and avoid looking vulnerable.*

Use the Buddy System: *Whenever possible, travel with a friend or in a group, especially at night or in unfamiliar areas.*

Have a Safety Plan: *Develop a safety plan for different situations, such as what to do if you feel threatened or harassed.*

Carry a Personal Safety Alarm: *Consider carrying a personal safety alarm that you can use to draw attention to yourself if you feel threatened. You can buy them on Amazon and other online retailers.*

Learn Basic Self-Defense Techniques: *Take a self-defense class to learn basic techniques for defending yourself in case of an attack.*

Be Mindful of Your Drinks: *When at a party or social gathering, never leave your drink unattended. If you feel unwell or suspicious after drinking, seek help immediately.*

*Use **Strong Passwords:** Protect your online accounts and personal information by using strong, unique passwords and enabling two-factor authentication where available.*

*Be **Cautious with Social Media:** Be mindful of the information you share on social media platforms, and adjust your privacy settings accordingly.*

*Lock **Doors and Windows:** Secure your home and car by locking doors and windows when you are inside or away.*

*Have **Emergency Contacts:** Always carry emergency contact information with you in case of an accident or emergency.*

*Avoid **Flashy Displays of Valuables:** Avoid drawing unnecessary attention to expensive items like jewelry, electronics, or cash.*

*Trustworthy **Transportation:** When using ride-sharing services or taxis, verify the driver's identity and the vehicle before getting in.*

*Know **Emergency Numbers:** Familiarize yourself with emergency numbers in your area and how to access help quickly.*

Remember, the goal of self-defense is to stay safe and avoid dangerous situations whenever possible. If you ever find yourself in a dangerous or threatening situation, try to de-escalate the situation and seek help immediately. Taking steps to protect yourself and being proactive about your safety can go a long way in ensuring your well-being.

Part Three: Advocating for Transgender Rights

Advocating for transgender rights as a transgender man can be a powerful way to make a positive impact and create change. Here are some ways you can be an advocate:

Share Your Story: *Share your personal experiences as a transgender man with others, whether through social media, blogs, or public speaking. Humanizing the transgender experience can help raise awareness and promote understanding.*

Support Transgender Organizations: *Get involved with local or national transgender organizations that focus on advocacy, support, and education. Volunteer your time, skills, or resources to contribute to their efforts.*

Educate Others: *Offer educational workshops or presentations on transgender issues and rights. Providing accurate information can dispel myths and misconceptions about transgender individuals.*

Participate in LGBTQ+ Events: *Attend LGBTQ+ events, Pride parades, and rallies to show solidarity and support for the community. These events often raise awareness and promote inclusivity.*

Engage in Policy Advocacy: *Advocate for transgender-inclusive policies at the local, state, and national levels. Write letters to legislators, participate in lobbying efforts, and join campaigns supporting transgender rights.*

Be Visible: *Live authentically as a transgender man and be visible in your community. Your visibility can challenge stereotypes and misconceptions.*

Use Social Media: *Use your social media platforms to share information, resources, and news related to transgender rights and* *issues. Engage with others in constructive discussions.*

Speak Out Against Discrimination: *Stand up against discrimination when you witness it, whether it's in public spaces, workplaces, or online. Be a vocal ally for those who face injustice.*

Empower and Support Others: *Offer support and encouragement to other transgender individuals and allies. Lend a listening ear and provide resources for those who may be struggling.*

Combat Stereotypes: *Challenge stereotypes and misconceptions about transgender people when you encounter them. Encourage others to learn and understand the diversity within the transgender community.*

Support Transgender Youth: *Advocate for inclusive policies in schools and support transgender youth in their educational journey. Speak out against bullying and discrimination in educational settings.*

Collaborate with Allies: *Work together with cisgender allies and other LGBTQ+ activists to amplify your advocacy efforts. Intersectional collaborations can strengthen your impact.*

Engage with Media: *Engage with media outlets to promote accurate and positive representations of transgender individuals and their experiences.*

Vote for Transgender-Inclusive Candidates: *Support political candidates who champion transgender rights and inclusivity in their platforms.*

Remember, advocacy can take various forms, and each person has their unique strengths and abilities to contribute. Whether it's through education, policy work, storytelling, or supporting others, your advocacy efforts can make a meaningful difference in the fight for transgender rights and equality.

CHAPTER TEN: CELEBRATING YOUR JOURNEY

Part One: Recognizing Personal Growth and Achievements

Recognizing personal growth and achievements as a transgender man is an important aspect of self-affirmation and building a positive self-image. Embracing your progress can boost self-confidence and provide motivation for further growth. Here are some ways to recognize and celebrate your personal growth and achievements:

Reflect on Your Journey: Take time to reflect on how far you've come in your gender affirmation journey. Consider the challenges you've overcome and the steps you've taken to become more comfortable and confident in your identity.

Celebrate Milestones: Celebrate the milestones you've achieved along the way, whether it's coming out to friends and family, starting hormone therapy, or living more authentically in your daily life.

Keep a Journal: Maintain a journal where you record your thoughts, feelings, and experiences related to your transition. This can serve as a valuable tool for tracking your progress and acknowledging your growth.

Set Personal Goals: Establish achievable and meaningful goals for yourself, both related to your transition and other aspects of your life. Celebrate when you reach these milestones, no matter how small they may seem.

Surround Yourself with Supportive People: Surround yourself with supportive friends, family, or members of the transgender community who can recognize and celebrate your achievements with you.

Practice Self-Compassion: Be kind to yourself and acknowledge that personal growth is a journey with ups and downs.

Celebrate your achievements, but also be gentle with yourself during challenging times.

Acknowledge Resilience: *Recognize your resilience and strength in navigating the obstacles and barriers you may encounter as a transgender man.*

Seek Professional Help: *If you're struggling to recognize your achievements or feeling overwhelmed, consider seeking support from a therapist or counselor who specializes in transgender issues.*

Compare with Yourself, Not Others: *Avoid comparing your journey to that of others. Everyone's path is unique, and recognizing your growth should be based on your own progress, not anyone else's.*

Embrace Positive Affirmations: *Incorporate positive affirmations into your daily routine. Remind yourself of your worth, value, and accomplishments regularly.*

Engage in Self-Care: *Take care of yourself and engage in activities that bring you joy and relaxation. Self-care is an essential part of recognizing personal growth and maintaining well-being.*

Educate Yourself: *Educate yourself about transgender experiences, history, and contributions to society. Recognizing the broader context of transgender existence can foster a sense of pride and empowerment.*

Remember that personal growth is an ongoing journey, and there is no set timeline for reaching certain milestones. Celebrate each step of progress, no matter how big or small, and remember that you are on a path of authenticity, courage, and self-discovery as a transgender man.

Part Two: Overcoming Challenges and Celebrating Resilience

Overcoming challenges as a transgender man can be a process that requires courage, resilience, and self-compassion. While each person's journey is unique, here are some strategies that may help you navigate and conquer challenges:

Seek Support: Surround yourself with a support network of friends, family, or members of the transgender community who understand and accept you for who you are. Connecting with others who share similar experiences can provide invaluable encouragement and validation.

Educate Yourself: Knowledge is empowering. Educate yourself about transgender issues, rights, and resources available to support you. Understanding your rights and knowing where to seek help can be crucial in overcoming challenges.

Find a Transgender-Affirming Healthcare Provider: Work with a knowledgeable healthcare provider experienced in transgender healthcare. Having a supportive healthcare team can assist in addressing medical and emotional needs related to your transition.

Practice Self-Compassion: Be kind to yourself and recognize that it's normal to face challenges. Give yourself permission to feel and process your emotions without judgment.

Set Realistic Goals: Break down larger challenges into smaller, manageable goals. Celebrate your achievements, no matter how small, as each step forward counts.

Prioritize Mental Health: Take care of your mental well-being by seeking therapy or counseling if needed. A mental health professional can offer valuable support and coping strategies.

Advocate for Yourself: Be your own advocate. Stand up for your rights and needs, whether it's in healthcare, education, or other areas of your life. Your voice matters, and speaking up can lead to positive change.

Establish Boundaries: Set boundaries with others to protect your emotional well-being. It's okay to limit interactions with people who are not supportive or respectful.

Engage in Self-Care: Make self-care a priority. Engage in activities that bring you joy, relaxation, and fulfillment. Taking care of yourself physically, emotionally, and mentally is vital in navigating challenges.

Celebrate Your Identity: Embrace your identity and be proud of who you are. Surround yourself with positive affirmations and reminders of your worth and value.

Educate Others: If you feel comfortable, educate others about transgender experiences and issues. Sharing your story can foster understanding and create a more inclusive environment.

Be Patient and Persistent: Overcoming challenges may take time, and setbacks are a normal part of the process. Be patient with yourself and stay persistent in working toward your goals.

Remember that you are not alone in facing challenges as a transgender man. There are resources, support groups, and organizations dedicated to assisting transgender individuals. Reach out for help when needed and remember that with time, effort, and a positive mindset, you can overcome challenges and thrive in your journey as your authentic self

Part of thriving in one's authentic self is by celebrating resiliency. Celebrating resilience is a wonderful way to acknowledge and honor your strength and ability to overcome challenges. Resilience is the capacity to bounce back from difficult situations and grow stronger through adversity. Here are some meaningful ways to celebrate your resilience:

Reflect on Your Journey: Take time to reflect on the obstacles you have faced and the challenges you have overcome. Recognize the progress you have made and the personal growth you have experienced.

Practice Self-Appreciation: Acknowledge and appreciate your efforts in navigating tough times. Celebrate your determination and courage in facing adversity.

Journal Your Triumphs: Keep a journal to document your journey of resilience. Write down the challenges you've overcome and the lessons you've learned along the way.

Share Your Story: Consider sharing your experiences with others. You never know how your story might inspire or empower someone else who is facing their own struggles.

Express Gratitude: Be grateful for the support and resources that have helped you during difficult times. Express gratitude to those who have been there for you on your resilience journey.

Engage in Self-Care: Celebrate your resilience by prioritizing self-care. Take time for activities that nourish your body, mind, and soul, such as spending time in nature, practicing mindfulness, or engaging in hobbies you enjoy.

Embrace Resilience Symbols: Choose a symbol that represents resilience to you and keep it as a reminder of your strength. It could be a piece of jewelry, a quote, or a meaningful object.

Set Goals and Celebrate Achievements: Set small, achievable goals for yourself and celebrate each accomplishment along the way. Recognize that progress is a result of your resilience and determination.

Surround Yourself with Positive Influences: Surround yourself with supportive and uplifting people who celebrate your resilience and encourage you to keep going.

Participate in Resilience-Building Activities: Engage in activities or workshops that focus on building resilience and coping skills. These activities can reinforce your ability to handle future challenges.

Practice Positive Affirmations: Use positive affirmations to remind yourself of your resilience and inner strength. Repeat affirmations that resonate with you regularly.

Be Kind to Yourself: Remember to be gentle with yourself. Recognize that everyone faces setbacks and challenges. Celebrate your ability to rise above difficulties, but also allow yourself to rest and recover when needed.

Celebrating resilience is not about dismissing the struggles you have faced but recognizing your capacity to endure and thrive despite them. Embrace your resilience as a source of empowerment and use it as a foundation for facing future challenges with confidence and determination.

Part Three: Contributing to the
Transgender Community

As a transgender person, you have a unique perspective and lived experience that can be incredibly valuable in contributing to the transgender community. Here are some meaningful ways you can make a positive impact:

Support and Mentorship: Offer support and mentorship to other transgender individuals who may be earlier in their journey. Your guidance and understanding can be a source of comfort and empowerment for those navigating similar experiences.

Share Your Story: Consider sharing your personal journey openly and authentically. Your story can help raise awareness, break down stereotypes, and foster understanding within and beyond the transgender community.

Advocate for Transgender Rights: Get involved in advocacy efforts to promote and protect the rights of transgender individuals. Support and participate in campaigns, initiatives, and organizations working toward equal rights and social acceptance.

Volunteer with Transgender Organizations: Contribute your time and skills to organizations that support and uplift the transgender community. Whether it's helping with events, outreach, or administrative tasks, your involvement can make a difference.

Provide Resources and Information: Offer resources, information, and support to transgender individuals seeking guidance on various aspects of their journey, such as medical care, legal rights, and mental health support.

Participate in Transgender Visibility Events: Be visible and participate in transgender pride events, marches, or local community gatherings. Your presence can inspire others and contribute to building a sense of community and belonging.

__Create Art and Media Representations:__ Use your creativity to produce art, writing, or media that showcases transgender experiences and challenges societal norms. Positive and accurate representations can foster empathy and understanding.

__Educate Others:__ Educate friends, family, colleagues, and others about transgender issues. Providing accurate information can dispel misconceptions and promote acceptance.

__Support Transgender-Inclusive Policies:__ Advocate for inclusive policies in workplaces, schools, healthcare settings, and public spaces. Support organizations that promote diversity and inclusivity.

__Be a Listening Ear:__ Offer a compassionate ear to transgender individuals who may need someone to talk to or share their feelings with. Being a supportive listener can make a significant difference.

__Collaborate with Allies:__ Collaborate with allies and other LGBTQ+ individuals to create a more inclusive and accepting society for everyone.

__Take Care of Yourself:__ Remember to prioritize self-care and well-being. Taking care of yourself allows you to better contribute to the community and inspire others.

Remember that each person's contribution can be meaningful, regardless of the scale. Whether through personal connections, advocacy efforts, or creative expression, your involvement in the transgender community can help create positive change and foster a more inclusive world.

CHAPTER ELEVEN: RESOURCES AND FURTHER SUPPORT

Part One: Books, Articles, and Online Sources

There are many excellent books, articles, and online sources that provide valuable information, support, and representation for transgender men. Here are some highly recommended resources:

Books:
- *"Trans Bodies, Trans Selves" edited by Laura Erickson-Schroth: A comprehensive resource guide covering a wide range of topics related to transgender health, well-being, and identity.*
- *"The Transgender Guidebook" by Anne L. Koch: A practical guidebook that covers medical, legal, and social aspects of transition for transgender individuals.*
- *"Ftm: Female-to-Male Transsexuals in Society" by Holly Devor: An in-depth exploration of the experiences and challenges faced by transgender men in society.*
- *"Transgender History" by Susan Stryker: A historical account of transgender experiences, activism, and identity in the United States.*
- *"The Testosterone Files: My Hormonal and Social Transformation from Female to Male" by Max Wolf Valerio: A memoir detailing the author's personal journey through transitioning.*

Articles:
- *GLAAD Transgender Resources: An extensive collection of articles and resources related to transgender issues, media representation, and advocacy efforts.*

- *Human Rights Campaign Transgender Visibility Guide: A guide that provides information on transgender visibility, rights, and allyship.*
- *National Center for Transgender Equality: An organization that offers a wealth of articles and resources on transgender rights, healthcare, and policy advocacy.*
- *Everyday Feminism Transgender Section: A collection of articles addressing various transgender-related topics from a feminist perspective.*
- *Trans Health at Fenway: A repository of articles and resources on transgender health and well-being.*

Online Sources:

- *Transgender Map: A comprehensive online platform that offers a wide range of resources, support groups, and information for transgender individuals.*
- *Transgender Legal Defense and Education Fund (TLDEF): A website dedicated to providing legal support and resources for transgender individuals.*
- *Reddit: There are various subreddits specifically for transgender individuals, such as r/ftm, where you can find supportive communities and discussions.*
- *The Trevor Project: An LGBTQ+ youth-focused organization that provides crisis intervention and suicide prevention resources.*
- *Transgender Pulse: An online forum where transgender individuals can connect, share experiences, and seek support.*

Please note that while these resources are reputable and helpful, it's essential to verify information and seek support from qualified healthcare professionals when making significant decisions about medical or legal aspects of transitioning. Additionally, the landscape of online resources can change, so keeping up-to-date with reputable sources is crucial.

Part Two: Support Groups
and Hotlines

There are several support groups and hotline numbers available for transgender individuals seeking help, resources, and a sense of community. Here are some reputable organizations and hotlines:

Support Groups:
- *Trans Lifeline: A non-profit organization providing peer support and crisis intervention specifically for transgender individuals.*
  Website: https://www.translifeline.org/
- *Gender Diversity: A support and educational organization for families, professionals, and transgender youth.*
  Website: https://www.genderdiversity.org/

- *Transgender Legal Defense & Education Fund (TLDEF): A legal organization offering support, resources, and advocacy for transgender individuals facing discrimination.*
  Website: https://transgenderlegal.org/
- *PFLAG (Parents, Families, and Friends of Lesbians and Gays): While not specifically transgender-focused, PFLAG offers support for LGBTQ+ individuals and their families.*
  Website: https://pflag.org/
- *Local LGBTQ+ Centers: Many cities and communities have LGBTQ+ centers that host support groups and provide resources for transgender individuals. Search online for LGBTQ+ centers near you.*

Hotline Numbers:

- *Trans Lifeline: A hotline staffed by transgender individuals for transgender individuals experiencing crisis or needing someone to talk to.*
US: 1-877-565-8860
Canada: 1-877-330-6366
- *The Trevor Project: A 24/7 crisis intervention and suicide prevention hotline for LGBTQ+ youth.*
US: 1-866-488-7386
Text "START" to 678678
Website: https://www.thetrevorproject.org/
- *National Suicide Prevention Lifeline: Not specific to transgender issues, but offers confidential support to anyone in distress.*
US: 1-800-273-TALK (1-800-273-8255)
- *RAINN (Rape, Abuse & Incest National Network): A national sexual assault hotline providing support for survivors.*
US: 1-800-656-HOPE (1-800-656-4673)
- *Crisis Text Line: A free, 24/7 text-based crisis support service.*
US: Text "HELLO" to 741741

Remember that reaching out for support is a sign of strength, and there are caring individuals and organizations ready to help. If you or someone you know is experiencing a crisis or struggling with mental health, don't hesitate to use these resources. You are not alone, and support is available.

Part Three: Finding Local
LGBTQ+ Services

Finding local LGBTQ+ services can be done through various methods. Here are some steps you can take to locate LGBTQ+ services and resources in your area:

Online Search: Use search engines to look for LGBTQ+ organizations, community centers, or support groups in your city or region. Use keywords such as "LGBTQ+ services in [your city]," "LGBTQ+ community center near me," or "transgender support group [your city]."

LGBTQ+ Directories: There are online directories specifically dedicated to listing LGBTQ+ resources and services. Websites like "The LGBT National Help Center" and "The Gay and Lesbian Switchboard" offer directories of LGBTQ+ organizations and helplines.

LGBTQ+ Community Centers: Check if your city or nearby areas have LGBTQ+ community centers. These centers often provide a wide range of services, including support groups, counseling, educational programs, and social events.

LGBTQ+ Organizations: Look for local LGBTQ+ organizations that focus on advocacy, support, or specific areas of interest, such as transgender rights, youth services, or healthcare.

LGBTQ+ Events and Pride Celebrations: Attend LGBTQ + events and pride celebrations in your area. These events often provide opportunities to connect with local LGBTQ+ community members and learn about available resources.

Local LGBTQ+ Publications: Check for LGBTQ+ publications or newspapers in your city or region. These publications often feature information about community resources and upcoming events.

LGBTQ+ Helplines: Look for LGBTQ+ helplines that offer support and information. Helplines can be valuable resources for finding local services and getting assistance when needed.

Social Media: Join LGBTQ+ groups or follow LGBTQ+ organizations on social media platforms like Facebook, Twitter, and Instagram. These platforms can be excellent sources of information about local events and services.

Ask Local LGBTQ+ Members: Reach out to local LGBTQ + individuals or friends to ask about resources and services available in the area. Personal recommendations can be valuable in finding supportive and safe spaces.

Healthcare Providers: Some doctors, therapists, or healthcare clinics may specialize in LGBTQ+ healthcare. They can provide information about local resources and support groups.

LGBTQ+ National Organizations: National LGBTQ+ organizations may have regional or local chapters that offer services in your area. Check their websites for local affiliates.

Remember to prioritize safety and confidentiality when seeking LGBTQ+ services. If you're not comfortable disclosing your identity right away, you can inquire about services without providing personal information. Additionally, be open to reaching out and exploring different resources to find the ones that best suit your needs and interests.

Conclusion

Congratulations! You have reached the conclusion of this guide on how to live as a transgender man. Throughout this journey, we have explored essential aspects of your identity, self-acceptance, navigating challenges, and celebrating your triumphs. As you embrace your authentic self, remember that living as a transgender man is a unique and courageous journey filled with growth, resilience, and self-discovery.

Understanding your transgender identity is the first step in this transformative process. By recognizing and accepting who you truly are, you have laid the foundation for a more fulfilling and authentic life. Embrace your journey with pride, and know that you are not alone. The transgender community is diverse, resilient, and ready to welcome you with open arms.

Navigating challenges and celebrating triumphs are an integral part of the transgender experience. Remember that resilience resides within you. You have already shown immense strength by acknowledging your truth and striving for a life that aligns with your identity. Embrace each step forward, whether big or small, for every achievement is a testament to your growth and determination.

As you move forward, continue seeking support from your chosen family, friends, or community. Surround yourself with those who uplift and accept you for who you are. Together, you can build a network of understanding and solidarity that fosters love, support, and growth.

It is essential to prioritize your mental and physical well-being on this journey. Accessing healthcare and professional support, along with addressing gender dysphoria, can be transformative for your overall happiness and self-assurance. Remember that your health and happiness matter, and you deserve to thrive in every aspect of your life.

Throughout this guide, we have explored the various ways you can contribute to the transgender community. By sharing your story, supporting others, advocating for rights, and embracing your unique perspective, you become an essential part of a powerful and diverse movement for equality and acceptance.

Finally, be kind to yourself and give yourself the grace to grow and evolve. Living authentically as a transgender man is an ongoing process, and it's okay to experience ups and downs. Cherish every moment of growth, and know that you are deserving of love, respect, and happiness.

As you continue your journey, remember that living as a transgender man is not just about overcoming challenges; it is about embracing your truth, living boldly, and inspiring others to do the same. You have the power to shape your narrative and create a world where all transgender individuals are celebrated and accepted for who they are.

Embrace your identity, celebrate your resilience, and continue writing your story—one that is full of strength, authenticity, and unwavering determination. You are not defined by society's norms; you are defined by the courage to be yourself, unapologetically and unreservedly. Live your truth, cherish your journey, and let your light shine brightly for all to see.

You are a remarkable force, and the world is better with you in it. Go forth and live as the incredible, authentic transgender man you are meant to be.

Printed in Great Britain
by Amazon

33136571R00050